University of East.

POETRY

MA Creative Writing
Anthologies 2014

UEA POETRY 2014

First published by Egg Box Publishing 2014

International ©2014 retained by individual authors

This book is sold subject to the condition that it shall not, by way of trade or otherwise, be lent, resold, hired out, stored in a retrieval system, or otherwise circulated without the publisher's prior consent in any form of binding or cover other than that in which it is published and without a similar condition including this condition being imposed on the subsequent purchaser.

A CIP record for this book is available from the British Library

UEA POETRY 2014 is typeset in Caslon. Titles are set in Din condensed, with subtitles in Gotham.

Printed and bound in the UK by Imprint Digital.

Designed and typeset by Sean Purdy.

Proofread by Sarah Gooderson.

Distributed by Central Books.

ISBN: 9780957661165

ACKNOWLEDGEMENTS

Thanks are due to the School of Literature, Drama and Creative Writing at UEA in partnership with Egg Box Publishing for making this anthology possible.

We'd also like to thank the following people:

Trezza Azzopardi, Amit Chaudhuri, Andrew Cowan, Giles Foden, Sarah Gooderson, Lavinia Greenlaw, Rachel Hore, Kathryn Hughes, Daniel Leeson, Michael Lengsfield, James Lasdun, Frances Leviston, Jean McNeil, Natalie Mitchell, Beatrice Poubeau, Sophie Robinson, Helen Smith, Henry Sutton, Val Taylor, Steve Waters, Peter Womack and Toby Young.

Nathan Hamilton at Egg Box Publishing and Sean Purdy.

Editorial team:

Michelle Brown
Susan K Burton
Niall Cunniffe
John Dennehy
Hannah Coneys
Affly Johnson
Ella Micheler
Lauren Razavi
Anealla Safdar
Rebecca White

CONTENTS

Introduction
Sophie Robinson—**07**

Contributors
William Annesley—**11**

Urvashi Bahuguna—**17**

Sam Buchan-Watts—**25**

Kate Duckney—**31**

A J Hodson—**39**

Affly Johnson—**47**

Madeleine Kruhly—**55**

Marena Lear—**61**

Jo Surzyn—**69**

Katie Swinson—**75**

James Sykes—**83**

Rebecca White—**89**

SOPHIE ROBINSON

Introduction

THIS IS MY FIRST YEAR AS A LECTURER AT THE UNIVERSITY OF EAST ANGLIA, and I am honoured to be able to introduce such an exciting body of work. It's been a pleasure to teach this talented bunch of poets, and a delight to see their work change and strengthen, even in the short time I've known them. Teaching the MA workshop this year has been energising and exhausting in equal measure: each student brought their best work, born of their lives, their experiences, their interests and their hard work, to workshops each week, and whilst the work varies greatly in style and theme, each student treated the work of their peers with respect and admiration. Moreover, what these poets share is a commitment to making the familiar new, to discovering fresh forms, original images, strange and wonderful new modes of expression.

What I enjoy the most about William Annesley's work is his reduction of the physical world, time and space, to the poem itself, its subjective lyric interiority. The final lines of 'Burn it into', for example, reduce both time and space to a private missive between speaker and subject: 'Flatten the space around the moment over and over again until it becomes Lick / its back and post it to me'.

Urvashi Bahuguna's poetry is meditative, dreamy, almost imagist in its stark simplicity. As such, one of Bahuguna's real strengths as a writer is her ability to compose precise, focused and highly original imagery. From the beautifully specific 'bangle' which 'hangs like a lantern' in 'Space' to the ominously vague 'thing more real than a word' in 'The Kite Runner', these poems present us with highly original yet understated imagery throughout.

Sam Buchan-Watts has a particular gift for making the familiar new. His poems bring an eerie new life to the domestic, the everyday;

INTRODUCTION

the 'collapsing futon', that perennial living room fixture, gains agency and menace, 'angling itself back / like a sexless wave'. There's a pleasing mistrust of nostalgia in this work: even the photograph, possibly the ultimate embodiment of nostalgia, is problematised, treated with suspicion, even: 'one ear of my dog is serendipitously / folded back forever'.

Kate Duckney's poems are marked with a distinctive aesthetic style, particularly through her use of gaps and lacunae within lines. The hesitancy or splitting of voice and language created by this technique is mirrored in the themes of the poems, particularly the recurring negotiation of the relationship between women and nature present in many of the poems featured here. The speaker in these poems often seems torn between the desire for symbiosis between herself and nature and a recoiling from the effacing of agency such pastoral desires might bring, resulting in a fracturing of self: 'a small colossal song of splitting, joining'.

A J Hodson's sequence of poems takes us through the latter days of a dying man's life with a great deal of skill and subtlety. Through the use of a variety of techniques, Hodson manages to convey a deep sense of loss and sadness without tipping into cliché or hyperbole. Rather, death is present in the everyday, the domestic: the 'shower curtain / [gliding] around his bed' mimicking the final curtain of the crematorium, 'automated / leisurely circling the coffin'.

Affly Johnson's poems concern themselves often with the lyric moment: the possibilities (and impossibilities) of capturing the specificities of a particular time and place engraved into memory through language. This results (amongst other things) in some wonderfully original imagery, from the stark directness of '[t]here are bits of your hair in the bin' to the more abstract 'biting the pastry arches of our home'.

There's an exquisite sense of character throughout Madeleine Kruhly's poetry. One of Kruhly's real strengths as a poet is her ability to paint a detailed and vivid lyric portrait of a person in a very small and sparse space of words. From the 'bulging throat' and 'thickplaid vest' in 'The Photo of Ken' to the esoteric phrases in 'In the morning', Kruhly's poems are littered with vivid subjectivities, painted with grace, humour and love.

Marena Lear has a lyric gift for enveloping the big within the small. From the 'intricate galaxies of movement' contained within the dancing bodies of 'Tango' to the 'three years and five time zones' separating the

SOPHIE ROBINSON

speaker from her memories in 'Through the Window', Lear manages gracefully to contain universal themes within the specific intricacies of daily life.

There's an incurable subtlety and complexity of human emotion present in Jo Surzyn's poetry. Always implied and never named, the emotions present in Surzyn's work show themselves through image and turn of phrase, from the ominous final image of 'template for a storm' to the slippage between subject and object (through the image of a packet of rotting fruit) in 'pipping'. These are precise, sparse and perfectly pitched poems, designed to take our breath away.

Katie Swinson's work concerns itself often with the relationship between present and past, particularly in relation to knowledge and understanding. As such, Swinson's poems are often placed between two temporalities, the speaker's hindsight providing a counternarrative to a past experience, managing to look backwards and forwards at once, suspended, skilfully, between two or more places and times. Swinson also plays with our subjective experience of time: the present tense of 'The Block at Evening Time' gives us a sense of continuity, the endless stretch of domestic time we experience as children.

James Sykes develops a pleasingly complex lyric speaker within his poems, often treading a thin line between humour and vulnerability, irony and the confessional: 'at the buffet table / feeling violent, feeling stupid, feeling ugly, feeling inappropriately erotic eating a falafel wrap'. There's a real and raw humaneness to Sykes's rendering of the lyric self in these poems, pleasing and moving in turn, and intensely readable too.

Rebecca White's lyric representations of time and memory are as complex as they are moving. The unique temporality of dreams is represented beautifully in 'The Garden', the speaker aware even in sleep of 'the future that has not yet happened'. Specificities of place are also beautifully rendered; one gets the sense throughout these poems of a decidedly non-nostalgic yearning, a desire of the speaker to return or remain in fleeting times and spaces, to 'stuff the landscape up [her] nose' or to find the now-absent lover, 'closer than [she] thought'.

There's so much more to these poems than these short introductory paragraphs will allow me to express, but I'll let you find that out for yourselves. These writers, through the skills, talents and hard work they've each put into their writing this year, bring new worlds to life on the page. My life is certainly richer for having read these poems, and I hope yours is too.

Sophie Robinson
Lecturer in Creative Writing

WILLIAM ANNESLEY

Burn it into

I can't write on trains

sea and

Sometimes I forget

ASSORTED POEMS

Burn it into

It is hot today
just like that other day when it was hot
The grass is still
so cold across the pavilion and I scan a spot
of lawn that has been quiffed into the fifties
been given the Elvis-blow-dry look by a zephyr
that can barely be felt

I want to squat on its face
and wear the dew on my legs like how the sweat clamours
under the duvet after sex in the Pyrenees heat

If my hair were a wig
I would take it right off
I   take   off

I'd let you blow on my brain even though
the sight of all those capillaries would make you vomit straight into it
The thought of being your ceramic toilet bowl
just for a second makes me cool

I feel self-conscious
looking into the eyes of the reflected version of myself that is petrified in
your sunglasses   I'd rather see you

Those glasses were probably designed for someone with a much bigger head and besides you could slap me on a postcard if only you would squint me two dimensionally

Flatten the space around the moment over and over again until it becomes Lick
its back and post it to me

WILLIAM ANNESLEY

I can't write on trains

When you try and compose yourself for a shit
on a train travelling faster than the last big
mac took to turn from a hoofed warm cow to
a flat warm meal it is a form of escape unlike any other. or until

that grey box behind your head, made to look
like a single square cereal sadly floating on
a plain of sour milk because the walls are yellow
but cold, tells you something about your fate like you should
eat your last meal or: 'hi this is paul

your crewleader speaking, the next station is
*your mother's womb, change here for the
umbilical cord'* and there are no sheep in that
field outside of your carriage B and the woman
punching tickets looks fondly at the toothless old
scottish man because his dog reminds her of the
child she hasn't had yet,

but I could be wrong.

sea and

The sea looks better than
your boyfriend. Don't feel
bad that salt
attracts you
more than stubble.

Film the way the wave sucks
the sand, the surf desperate
to be

more than a product
of the moon's dislocating haul

the temperance of rotation
cannot be masked in ten seconds
of personal broadcast

Does your boyfriend gravitate?

Froth at the
lip?

Make cool?

Melt   your heart? Your battery life
barely musters a phone call anymore and here

you are snapping.

WILLIAM ANNESLEY

Sometimes I forget

OK so when we

begun to paint

each other, on each other's skin,

the soft powder pigment licking your

belly button eased by water and emulsifying cotton fluff that was

partly yours and partly the remnants of sleeping in my blue cotton

boxer shorts for three nights in a row, I made branches on you. Roots grew

out from panty line – I hate that word – the dip where your hip bone stretches

skin like a cool wave. You hooked your arms neat through the hitches

in my armpit and the underbrush that lay between

our torsos rhythmically seasoned.

And without rubbing you off the A4 paper I was given yesterday

in a class of us, I do feel as though you tore

up the image last night in between the 7th shot of

malibu and the mark I left with the corner of the aftershave against

two walls in my bedroom.

You are beautiful in peroxide now

slightly off balance as if I taught you how to walk pigeon-toed like I

ASSORTED POEMS

was shown in vhs by the knee doctors. We sleep easy

naked and the mornings are always the skin of us

under the nail of us. Without rips in your jeans or paint in between the frown

lines that carve through google maps we probably wouldn't

feel strong dressed how we want to dress. Lip me tightly

In between the rem moments where you forget your arm in me.

William Annesley is a London-based poet who addresses the concepts of memory and identity in his work through an exploration of an emotional ambiguity to certain life events. The ambiguity arises out of the dichotomy between true and false memory, which he attempts to engage with and learn from only through the process of creating a self-contained lyric space.

URVASHI BAHUGUNA

Space

daughter

The Kite Runner

Teach me how to ghazal

The naming of daughters

Shorelines

Space

The handle on your tea cup
is painted blue & tinted green
by falling light,

your two fingers loop
through its ear-shape
curve.

Your bangle hangs like a lantern
on your wrist and there is room enough
to carry a flame.

A darkening of autumn leaves
between your breasts,
a shadowhold.

When you press your feet together like hands,
the gaps let in grass mud sunlight.

At night you lie palm first on my chest,
your legs knot tightly
around mine and the spaces disappear.

daughter

you come from a long line
of elms
who have housed hummingbirds
and runaways

take women in
from the rain
and clothe them

in the cool cloister
of your bark

give them
branches as arms
to raise in prayer

they will help you age with grace
every wrinkle
a year folded into yourself

the monsoon will draw pools
at your feet

the wind will clear the quiet

daughter
you are freer than you know

The Kite Runner

I swallowed a word from a story
charcoal in my lungs

the word was *kohl*

on the eyes of
a dancing boy

four palms tall

his skirt
creating circular canopies

in my head
as he turned

his face finding mine
holding it by his bangled wrists

before a man pulled him away
to learn

a thing more real than a word.

URVASHI BAHUGUNA

Teach me how to ghazal

the curve of your palm
on the small of my back
other hand
holding mine in place

you lead
my feet have always followed
where water has already
charted the course

dance with me
feet bare
where it began
as rain struck the ground
and ghazals were written
by men drunk on the scent of wet earth

ASSORTED POEMS

The naming of daughters

is a habit
sown into our palms,

rivulets ridged

long before the
foretelling of flood.

The first name
I chose belonged
to a geisha

Mameha
for a daughter who would ripple,
ring following ring in open water:
Ma me ha

Naintara
and *Moraya*
will be my
twin homages
to the night
I was born

with a name
like *ghungru* bells ringing thrice.

Naintara is an Indian name that means star of my eyes, my beloved.

Moraya is a little known moon goddess worshipped in Armenia.

Ghungru bells are bells attached to anklets worn by dancers in classical Indian dance forms. My name comes from a mythological dancer from the heavens.

URVASHI BAHUGUNA

Shorelines

The hummingbird belongs to the tree, but the drummer is every part earth.
I have followed mud like the black seeds of a kiwi
pulsating towards the white interior.
Travelled inland following
tin drums below the surface.

When the thirst first came to me,
I was a decade old under the sea's tutelage.

They sing of me in dark quarters,
they sing of me when the night is old.

How I cannot swim in waters
deeper than me,
my heart beating the enemy's drum when I venture close
to the descent.

I am a popular legend of the edge-lands, the horror I strike
is not easy to come by here. I have never swum with a whale,
I collect starfish and follow crab trails.

If I was not coloured by the sun, they would not believe
I was from the edges.

My people can see under water
they see the darkness move, they say night has nothing on it.

I used to wear the traditional black paint
on my feet.
But not having seen the darkness I do not deserve its markings.

There is a man who lives further from the water
than the rest. The lines on his forehead receding like the shorelines,
high tide, low tide.

ASSORTED POEMS

Sometimes, he sings
and the sea & the lands
accompany him,
neither hearing the other.

Urvashi Bahuguna has had poetry previously published in *The Four Quarters Magazine, Muse India, The Cadaverine* and elsewhere.

SAM BUCHAN-WATTS

Nose to Tail

The Dogs

The Sacks

Matters Concerning God

collapsing futon

Nose to Tail

in places far from here, and colder
– like the northern US states Wisconsin, or Alaska –
pigs can freeze to the sides of trucks or have
their limbs crushed by other pigs' limbs

At a gridlock somewhere in North Norfolk
a two-tier truck of livestock waits next to a school bus.
The spotted pigs in the upper tier could be oinking
the most enormous racket, but the bus is icy private
like a cool-box, and from the top deck all you can do
is glance through the slit where the angle makes
the dark pale and mottled rug of upright pigs
inside have no apparent end. In fact,
it is quite difficult to know exactly where one pig stops
and another begins, and the shape of other pigs
in the lattice of pink flesh
make each individual pig's expression seem a smirk
at being privy to this sequestered mass,
chuffed with the pure occasion of it.

SAM BUCHAN-WATTS

The Dogs

I dreamt my most cherished photographs
were all transformed overnight into those of dogs:
big horny dogs in their ripest years
hogging the frame for themselves.

Every last photographer's trick employed
so that even in the tacky studio where he couldn't focus
my dog, like a good dog, looks ever curious and propositional
baring his hunk of incisor at us, its nourished decay.

In the more rough cut alfresco shots with an arty contrast
between negative and positive textures, my black dog
merges with the dark or slides into a pond in such a way
that dog and pond are seamless.

In this dream world one ear of my dog is serendipitously
folded back forever, fixed there,
and though the tawny insides appear knobby and esoteric
they indicate a constant alertness to any thrown ball

or that he is newly ruffled from rolling in the buzzing grass.
There is a version of the choice photo stashed in my wallet,
its creased folds now powdery with a private friction;
his profile is divine against a backdrop of swirling marble blue.

This day I remember for its stressful hilarity; we could not bundle his legs
onto the stool. Since then the dog has been as mute
as the pictures. Perhaps somewhere
in his cropped-out lower throat, his bark is stuck.

The Sacks

A new dilemma is nesting in our homes, the kitchens, living rooms.
It will make us clamber like lobsters in the dark; boil our shoes and eat them.

And still we keep stashing them in whole networks of sacks
hyper-breeding to the humming gyrate
of my fridge. Now there are stacks
and that sterile whiff when you get near to asphyxiate,

in the crevice between dishwasher and chipboard-unit.
Magicked to hover there, just above the floor's chill,
where other increments of us sit,
dust, dead flies, dandruff – the homely filth.

They rest without tension, raised a smidgen
like the gossamer fur of soya beans,
a sleep shirt slipping from a girl's chest;
ominous and looming as B-movie graveyard mist.

SAM BUCHAN-WATTS

Matters Concerning God

We kept you at arm's reach like a birthday cake.
I never saw your fury or your drunk face.
Now the only matter I can picture
is opaque: the soft pink bellow of sun in your ears.

'Are you not jealous of other people's things – on the bus
ride home, of their cars?' There was your calm rebuff,
but that didn't matter. I still keep
the view of your kitchen from the porch

the hot, halogen hall, your father's chide over grades
from off-stage, and the way the lamps upstairs unite.
Then the dingy corners, the ancient filth and other matter,
places the skylight cannot reach. Maybe that's where you prayed.

collapsing futon

There is something unspeakably sad
about the collapsing futon
angling itself back
like a sexless wave
the way it continues to spill its
pillows
and the knackered slats
with their nagging tendency
to slide.
The futon is untenable
it needs to be dragged
by its claws across laminate flooring
like a disobedient dog is dragged to bed.
I make my mind stark and itemless
with the gloss of a new gallery.
The futon persists
trying to look relaxed
and relaxing.
I choose not to stare
and while my attention is fixed elsewhere
the futon is placed in a van
driven by a man I do not recognise
and draped over with a specially-designed futon cover.
A screw or something more instrumental
is pulled from the base of its spine
the futon slides to its shins
then over on its side.

Sam Buchan-Watts is a founding editor of the *Clinic* anthology series, and poetry editor of *Five Dials* literary magazine. His work has appeared in *The Best British Poetry 2013* (Salt) and elsewhere.

KATE DUCKNEY

In the cathedral garden

Visions

Orlando

My little symbol

You Say

Narcissa

ASSORTED POEMS

In the cathedral garden

        tore my red hair in the willow dreads   said for *nests, for nests*
but really for another's dark shock   God I want to move in a different dream time God I want
   the priests whose bedrooms overlook this garden to see how a woman's body looks
    when she comprehends being puffed out of rib dust   the chalk eraser slam on slam
    of man   I suppose I look like I don't know how I got here   I suppose I'm asking
                       whose thistlemilk I sucked

in the royal barn cool of cloisters I feel it more   hot core in the humble column of me
               and without knowing how to pray I prayer-maze it out
    (just seeing, just trying)   unfair how it juts and grows   the bone snowflake
                         that builds me, unfair!

an ash tray on every round table, I ask you   and a wire-crutched sapling beside it   tell me who
is crooning *kill* into the fruit heavy morning? and who   believes I would not sooner starve
        than slip that frog bright berry in my mouth   let them wait
                       at their windows

Visions

I don't dream about my teeth falling out but I do
dream that circles of not-men with coneshaped skulls
push me down on pelt to force fangs
through my nipples, grin freezing on the skin rug.

Our bed smells like a domesticated bird. The answer
through seedwarm hair is always 'you –
we were in this kitchen and one thing led to –'
hiding my father's hand in a sunshine yellow cereal box;

spread out on a wasp-carpet, fading in their alkaline, smiling;
I know the aurora borealis is in the sky above me
but I'm not looking. You say it into what I see. Falling
from a dark shelf like the limits of a racing game, again:
I know the aurora borealis –

ASSORTED POEMS

Orlando

can I take myself to the edge and forget myself   when myself is a gleam in a leg crook
a dent between hinges   while the water makes me   lovely, lovely   catching the kind of light
that kindles   diamond cool   on submarine walls

even when there is nothing   and nobody   to know a beauty   in hills where the shadowplay
of high hawks ripples over stone   and a wind tries to teach me
which breaches in my body it should blow through
the hollows that whistle   and ache   the valves that blink sealed   on a day   like today

where I have myself   featureless as the face of prayer
on these heights above the houses   the tucked, breathless village
in its warped smallness against the green   *like whalebone*   I feel myself think
as the wind falls flat   inside igneous combs of marrow
like whalebone

KATE DUCKNEY

My little symbol

Roseburn   thorngasp   the first
stone pestle feeling of being filled
leg hooking
spider shy
over his back
as if appearing
from a silver drain

room makes body   instead of love   that known and clouded candle
she feels   the pulsing textures of the ceiling
from the skating apostrophes   of light in eye corners
and when   she turns her head
rain is fibre optic on the needles of pines
each drop the vividness in the charge   of her veins
yes   and the heart its real shape
the knotted stump
and stunted fins of it

ASSORTED POEMS

You Say

there are kids in America soaking tampons in vodka and there are kids in America so high they believe their girlfriend's faces are portals to planetariums I mean imagine thinking you'd spluttered the spot of Jupiter into a waste paper basket how wonderful to get no service in a restaurant because for one night you are the devil my love how far have you ventured into the Other Side Of YouTube tonight would you not rather sit with me would you not rather live a little who are these people and what is a weed song why would you want to die listening to one I can tell you that teleporting to an alien tongue makes you chew on your own and it's surprisingly great you are a continuous example of the present continuous it was you who made me see how the sea at night can be there all the time when the light is not shining yes in fact I see so much through you and your blue-lit silence your back where the bones bar like a shadow of a jail door closing let's drink something let's fuck in a place where there's ivy and crisp packets from the 90s all faded I don't mind I could talk into that look you give me all night you are so much like that galaxy print all the kids are wearing

KATE DUCKNEY

Narcissa

It can begin   with the spring tint of wet wings   a certain nettleness
beneath the snow of them   and when I tug the rough tongues of grass   burred
with duckwing dew beads   and cuckoo spit   I know as I know anything   I will find it
a root   the gradient green into white
and no one to hear how the bite of newness   echoes

A honey-trust so thick   that something whirring   has settled on the salt
of the clothes I peeled in the peace forest   wanting as I have wanted lately
to see my picture on the pond again
a look in the wrinkled veins light into food   light into youngest amber
and a wild thought only a body could think   and display like a bud

No, I cannot crash through the algae for it   I am better
with my hand on myself, the word other on my mouth
like the call unquestioned   from the pairing throats in branches
a small colossal song of splitting, joining

Kate Duckney was the 2013 recipient of the Ink, Sweat and Tears scholarship and the Poetry-Next-The-Sea prize for best creative dissertation. Her main poetic preoccupations currently include misandry, fluids, cuckoo spit, the colour black, cyborg pregnancy and the disappearance of the female body.

A J HODSON

Closing
Overarching title for this collection

I. The Method Actor
II. The Conversation
III. The Raincheck
IV. A Ward
V. The Draught Excluder
VI. The Receptacle

I. The Method Actor

The talent in his liver was late to bloom.
Before the script could wilt in his grip,
he wafted Rigor Mortis up through it,
from bottom to top, until it stood quite straight.

His eyes tiptoed along the page's crest
that seemed a countdown's
length of sparkler or fuse.
As you can see, it's bad news I'm afraid.

He'd been here before, but spotted
the full stop of tumour in the scan
quicker than the rumour of the baby
in ultrasound. *Are you sure it's there?*

The doctor knew from the start
he was perfect for the background role of 'Dying Man Number Two',
was born for it,

even though he could only
grasp a fistful of air where they said
she was, the almost-widow not yet cast struggling to remember her lines,

while a nurse showed him how to throw himself on his sword, then said:
You can take it from here. From then on,
he performed all his own injections

while on his belly the coddled
water bottle lay frankly like an Olivier Award
coercing him into limelight to say:
For this honour, I'd like to thank...

II. The Conversation

It's all laid out.

A crumpled tissue, where you keep it
down your sleeve, shows itself,
exposed like the frill of a splash
captured among the breaker rocks.

Telling the family soon.

It was never in a conch,
this surge of sea. In your ear
you were lugging for the moon,
damn it, to do its job.

Packing up the pieces now.

Practising an expert tug of tablecloth
from under the coastal town,
waving away the crumbs
of picnic onto the pebbles.

Something but bones for the gulls.

Ignoring the froth of doilies washing
in, the napkins squawking overhead,
the castles toppling for toddlers, he's learning
how to walk again towards the dismantling town.

Flapping sandals wish to talk.

The folding cafés and tea rooms there
that never wash up on the sands.
Is the right time to tell them when the tide
is going out or coming in?

I'll be picking up the pieces then.

III. The Raincheck

The drains can't swallow such truth.
Here it comes, just as they said it would.
Sometimes you can see wind's arms
brushing it aside, forcing a path
through the crowd, going ahead.

As drizzle wets the cars, homeowners
shut their windows like eyes at an end
not yet arrived. Inside, a family is closing
ranks. Outside, Olympic rings link
in puddles stepped in by wellingtons.

Sloshing alone through the rain, a man
lowers the hood of his mackintosh,
uplifts his head, sticks out his tongue.
Here it comes, an image of heavy rain
dropping through his skeleton.

IV. A Ward

On the way in, there's the soap
dispenser at the door helping us
to wash our hands of him.

There's something certain
about the nurse
bearing the bedpan

to his room as she says
he'll be with you shortly
and something unfamiliar

about the shower curtain
she glides around his bed.
We'll see it sometime later,

at the crematorium, automated,
leisurely circling the coffin
like a tour guide's route.

A loo flushes and the nurse emerges
removing the sagging old fruit
we brought him the last time.

He just couldn't eat it, she admits
as she drags the curtain aside,
and he's mostly brought back,

propped up in the adjustable bed,
and we're mostly there too and we're
on the way out, upholding deadpan faces

and ignoring the soap.

V. The Draught Excluder

There's wind in the chimney
like breath down a neck.
As the door opens a crack,

then pushes wide, it swipes an arc
across the carpet, hisses
as an excluder rides the wave

of the draught that will squeeze
in from under the door
to walk all over his grave.

Two male nurses have come
wide with smiles full of gaps
they can whistle through

to visit him and his bed full of air.
They empty his catheter,
give the closest of shaves,

every week share the burden of care
with his wife, then leave the excluder
where it was pushed, to the wall.

A J HODSON

VI. The Receptacle

You asked and I opened the hinged oak lid expecting a whole man jack-in-the-boxed but found only the ash of him. The usual disappointment of a package wrongly dispatched came rushing back, as if I'd been sent a box containing nothing but polystyrene and bubble wrap or the antique dust of a vase powdered in transit. No man there, no baroque ornament, just these fine, grey sleepers, each one of the trillion grains of him that mattered, laying down their afterlives to preserve the fragile, in absentia thing inside. That's why they can't be scattered.

A J Hodson was born in Cheltenham, Gloucestershire. An undergraduate studying English Literature with Creative Writing at the University of East Anglia, he was shortlisted for the Bridport Poetry Prize in both 2012 and 2013. This collection is a tribute to his grandfather who died in 2010 of liver cancer.

AFFLY JOHNSON

Dad

Brecknock Gardens

Offerings

Côte d'Ivoire

Haircut

Pentewan

Dad

in winter when the ice-cream comets
fret the beetles you seek the organic
muddy carrots and the bare bones of things
I start   as the younger hunter
possesses your skin
the pullus in a store cupboard nest
perpetually in a state of eat
biting the pastry arches of our home
I bring you grains in my boots but find sugar
paper stuffed under piles of your sweaters
Across the pea-podded courtyard you bare your teeth
and run for me   sliding
I've hidden your spikiest
shoes encasing your sneezes
After the shortest day
you can open your briefcase to
catch my seasickness
we eat chips and watch
the white blush of crocuses propped
up on your barrow full of onions

AFFLY JOHNSON

Brecknock Gardens

Sculling above the green
we kiss   the clipped fronds mottling between the blades of beard
electric dinghies roll concentric over the pond
running the boatman aground
Stubbing the grass, we roll back and forth to each other
laugh gasps and private thoughts suspended
in the upward swing
Rashy calved I pop a Piriton, picnic champagne sedative
mulls the cranial cavity and
I stay away from heavy machinery

Offerings

You've done your quota   thrown me the scraps
Like a sea lion I am dredged waiting for
mackerel and an ear
Your arm on my thigh cinches dull pain to the nerves
amplifying the distance
Static body and silence mix with the stomach acids
abrade the blubbery bags   sidling
through like 6 hour digest   like a Happy Meal all carb
and punishment and latent hunger
But I welcome the static and silence and roll over
I'll wake to wine injuries on my shins and you'll lick
my cheek in
such a way that starts the ventricles and
serotonin   It's Narnia with you   wrapping
me in jokes and dripping denim
I wish we could communicate
but your irises are flirting over mine
the coquette's white flag waving
in their sockets
rendering me animal

AFFLY JOHNSON

Côte d'Ivoire

There is Africanness in the bits between

my bones between the areola sacks
My blood is hers it's brave blood but in the body

spaces I am black
between the toes, the curve
of my back but I only know plantains

their crispy discs and chipping
plate scum

the furtive licks that make me feel alien
paving the way for the dissension but that's later on
I have the stubbornness and calm of the new
husband   his love signature lassoed me like a tidal weed on the edge of
    the earth rooted and
bobbing
She stuffs the strange pepper
fabrics in high drawers till next year washing me
blended brown

Haircut

There are bits of your hair in the bin. The dregs of our weekend.
I cut it for you in the conservatory on Sunday
your mascara had jilted your eyes
in favour of your cheeks.
I wondered whether this is what it is like to be a mother.
Your infant dangling between 2 blades
each snip attempting refinement but
they keep splitting and growing back.

AFFLY JOHNSON

Pentewan

I ran to the rocks to splash my face
and found
the miner's son,
Jagger's water-muscle chest
and strutting arms.
His sweat, peat,
and grassy moor call rang.
His subject, I grappled for roots
in the earth.
Something lovable about the left handed;
thin grit
under his fingernails
and green weed lacing my shoes.
Propelled in our fray dance
my lady bird hem dips in pools
away from the mouth of the cave
The wellington boot Dune Haka
had us both
till pulled by the moontide
his grains shed to the cliff face
and I was left to the shallows.

Affly Johnson is an English graduate from UEA where she began to mine her personal life for poetry. She owes her time on the MA for the current explorations of femininity, ethnicity and ageing in her work and for making it louder and braver.

MADELEINE KRUHLY

Before Divorce

The Photo of Ken

In the morning

To fish

Child

Before Divorce

I paint the circle
green and think
it is ripe.

We cross our feet
near ant hills and
weeds

and the sheet of
paper stretches
in front

of our legs. We
draw without
stencils

while behind the
half-shutters of
our house

the two shadows
that move our
blood

bend and slice
like fine hooks

in the currents
rushing below
our heaviest
roof.

MADELEINE KRUHLY

The Photo of Ken

He smoked and his face
lushed, a sidewalk
after dark

while at the hour of five or
four my mother held him
in his study

gave lips to his left cheek and
did not notice the stain on
his lung

which posed in the middle,
wooden float in a stilled
lake.

Ken tried to cover it with
a wink and little weight
loss

hot bottle-fly hair wilting
as he was asked to stop
Ken please

empty your pockets and sink
those doe-branded silver
lighters.

His daughter buttoned
his thickplaid vest and
looped

ties around a bulging throat,
making him lemonade
bourbon and ice

while Ken was told you're
wasting Ken you're
wasted.

In the morning

Pong wakes early in the cold and knows it is warmer in China.
He freezes his nails under our faucet, and I see that it is still
blue outside. As he dresses in thin shirts, milk boils in the
pot and I think of throwing away satsumas. Will Pong
mind, does he like these bitter skins.

He steps down the stairs and opens the glass door like a thought
simple and slow. I will be late tonight, there is a project, oh
dear. I nod and give him an old orange for luck. Pong will
return before our meal and ask if I have had a good
dream. I will say that I have had this, the morning
in tempered ink.

To fish

One fisherman will recognize
another fisherman from afar

my babushka said. He knows
his second self by dock-bent
knees

or scales on sleeves, his
clothes webbed in oiled
spines

his joints aching as he
settles on sea-end
boards.

Like the fisherman, I feed
my hook and cast a rod
taking care

to dangle the line

while wondering if I will
be recognized by these
words

that are not yet dried
in salt, that are not
yet flesh.

Child

I leave in hours and
it is night and will
be night.

We watch tennis, the
two of us. Blue
court tennis.

She wants to drink
and does, wine
and water.

She rubs my back
like moon rubs
moon

and says I will love
you always, child.

I tilt to the east
and think she
will

but what if I can
not give a love
like that

of my own.

Madeleine Kruhly comes from the outskirts of Philadelphia, PA, where she completed her undergraduate degree in English Literature with a Creative Writing concentration at the University of Pennsylvania. She would like to thank her tutors and her fellow MA students for their hard work and inspiring words.

MARENA LEAR

Tango

Making Coffee

Noah

Portrait in Amber

Through the Window

The Beetroot

Tango

Like two atoms of a molecule, they approach
take their inevitable embrace, and begin
to follow an invisible vapor trail around the floor,
as if breathing into traces left by a star birth.

There is a point of stillness, a galactic nucleus, a silence so complete
between the two, it is heard: the sound of moon opening an eye
over a flushed desert. He can feel even the minutest tear
in her nylons, in the same way that, lying on the grass,
one senses the warmth enveloping each separate blade.

Now for the creation: the precise geometry
of each tiny collision, the way the foot can only remain
attached to the floor for so long before the step
dies, but out of each combustion blooms a new impulse,
born out of that namelessness that floats between, the urge
which precedes even desire, the speaking that is prelude to words.

Eventually, the beetle-black belly of the *bandoneón* will stop its heaving,
the violinist will abandon the bow for the water bottle. Fresh drinks clutched
to clammy hands, flux of laughter will accompany the shuffling of partners,
bra strap adjustments – all the little momentary intrusions of self.
But perhaps the message remains, hovering in shadows

over the dance floor, unseen intricate galaxies of movement
heaped in layers like fossils in rock strata; the musical notation
of prehistory, a kind of tangible evidence of the sublime
to be discovered eons from now – to be caressed, crooned at, understood
by some loving creature from another world.

MARENA LEAR

Making Coffee

My grandmother smooths the grounds
around the grim lip of the coffee maker,
screws on the squeaky top, and lights the stove
with one practiced flick of the hand.

Perched on stools in the kitchen, she preens me,
brushing a crumb from my blouse, examining
the hole in my earlobe she pierced herself
with an ice cube and a needle years ago;
a fishhook for an eager guppy finning towards
the waters of a world alien to her own.
She frowns at the sharpness of my collarbone,
says that men like women softer, fleshier,
with faces like the sea: smooth and placid
the morning after a hurricane.

Lipstick trickles through the cracks
around her mouth, but I don't tell her,
I just gesture at the coffee maker
which is now huffing and hissing
like the old widow next door on her evening walks.

She adds one, two, and a half
teaspoons of sugar, poised with the spoon
between her fingers, polished marble nails,
perfectly coiffed, smelling of White Diamonds
while I slouch in my jean shorts,
and together we sip, exhale, sip, exhale.

Noah

Days pass like drops in a naked eye;
the gray pestle-grind of light on wet boards

where he paces, blind and burning
to sustain the words in his mind

words which grow dull like agates
hoarded for too long in the same pocket.

The bloated hold below him groans
and sways with animal unease.

Hands on the wooden beams,
his bones are growing gnarled

he cannot tell their stench from his own,
his skin is stretched thin like tarpaulin,

it cannot hold, not forever, but
there are times he thinks he hears

in the brush of a wing against iron,
the bellow of a bull – a voice, perhaps –

but the waves come again to throw
their savage sound over his thoughts,

their moans more felt than heard,
like the dumb language of the stomach.

Night on the sea is darkest
because the shadows surge from beneath

to palm this earthly evidence
this floating cradle for the salt-mad man –

he rocks in the *slap slap* of water
a fitful infant lulled against its will

by the beat of a tyrannical heart.

Portrait in Amber

When we spoke of leaving
a wind shook in your eyes, scattering grains
over peaks of sand dunes,
the winter sky at once so dense a burden
your fingers had to loosen the spoon
to thunder against the plate grown pale
on the kitchen table.

When we spoke of
the leaving the sound sought refuge
in the air molecules, condensed into
a translucent sphere encircling
the table, the chairs, the plate, the spoon,
the dying succulent your aunt gave you,
its leaves frostbitten into fingernail shards.

When we spoke
the words fell off the stems
rusted iron filings blown from lips
the last twitches of movement
in sap-caught insect limbs:
when we
      when
           w
                e

ASSORTED POEMS

Through the Window

It is winter now in Buenos Aires, and the gutters of Avenue Corrientes
will be choking on the last leaves like gas-soaked rags
below your building where we laid on that dirty mattress on the roof,
passing a joint, pouting lips and inhaling the too bright stars
alive and more distant than ever from one another.

Three years and five time zones away, I try to recall
singing chacareras with the folk musician who was missing two teeth;
locking ourselves in your room for three days with a broken air conditioner,
and your guitar resting in the corner, blushing deeper
in the window's changing light, like something in a Márquez novel.

We suck these images down to the last drop
(the wine we drank at the corner bar but never paid for,
walking out into the night, two cockeyed pigeons)
so that we are never too sober to analyze the next one,
and we stumble on, and every step brings us to a center point.

On the mirror side of the seasons, a cat wanders rooftops
and two lovers sit on a park bench flipping a coin.

The Beetroot

Gnarled heart of Beta
rough bumped through
the ages, clay-warmed first
in Eve's naked fist, then
cradled in shaded soil
black pearl in an earlobe
rolled through labyrinthine
hanging gardens sheltering sugared light.
in a dirt clod

MARENA LEAR

*

Wrenched from
deeper earth
to cut, pulsing oil red
rings of crystalline like
petroleum tributaries urging
circular return to blood –
a taste that should be salt
but sweetens dizzy.
You yield to a child's wisdom
sucking on a gravel-sliced knee
the comfort of touching tongue
to the bright bloom,
eyes closed, almost swooning
the color numinous
in the cave of your mouth.

*

To open is to bear
wide-eyed witness
to the battlefield inside:
the troubled waves and gutted sun
a pictograph in a time capsule
divulging the brave and bloody history
of a distant purple planet.

Marena Lear was born in Havana, but has lived most of her life in different parts of the Pacific Northwest of the US, land of pine trees, Nirvana, and delicious coffee. She has immensely enjoyed this fruitful year of writing, and appreciates having had the opportunity to get to know this group of talented and passionate writers.

JO SURZYN

letters to composer

template for a storm

Friday, Late

pipping

I hear these voices that will not be drowned

letters to composer

how delicious the reed beds look in this light
and the river as it laps the boardwalk

      it's over an hour
on foot to the church, just to slip
into the nave, test a voice
against the cool stone walls and back again
              it's a unique thirst
                      this endless beaching

          i passed a ship
and it sounds romanticised, i know
but she really was called the enchantress
                        it's all this music

i should confess, i've been playing
two-part harmonies on your piano
and all these moments, i've been thinking
                    i'd like to call them minims

     in the mornings
i've been sizing the bites in the broccoli leaves
against my own unmeasured tongue

      will you sing me a full stop
i'd like to hear you voice the pause of it
                    just for a minim

JO SURZYN

template for a storm

I can only picture being in hurricanes
on still nights when no hurricanes can happen.
The first night I spent in one was my second alive –
I'm in the stories quite a lot and I can't tell a single one.
Sometimes I confuse helicopters

for the wind picking up. I have a blueprint
of our street furniture and where it might fall
should those not be helicopters after all. Our bedroom
lies between an electric pylon and a telephone pole
and yes, this bothers me in bad weather
but it was quiet as I slept

   and dreamt of a woman

      I knew but didn't recognise

         she was cutting my hair

           and I told her

        she could do anything she wanted

and the wind that woke me up
could've cleaved a house in two.

Friday, Late

To call it a shoal would be overstated –
it was really only two or three
glints of light across the tiles
but they were distinctly silver
and their movement – as if swimming –
led me to name them *The Silver Fish*.

By morning, I did not believe this moment
had really happened, so when I told you, I told you
as if it were a dream, and you said *typical*
which I thought meant typical of me.

JO SURZYN

pipping

orange turns
talc white
in the fruit bowl
evolves
to the bluegreen
of capillaries
hold your wrist
close
do you see it

before
I can
bring myself
to slip
a finger through
the skin
you've hauled the whole net
to the bin
like so many fish

ASSORTED POEMS

I hear these voices that will not be drowned

I know I should turn back
to my hotel room, to the loyalty
of the kettle, the toilet, the TV

but I'm calling this a pilgrimage
you can't go there and not see it

so I will take a photo on my phone
to prove I got there and I saw it
and I'll leave my phone and its photo and my clothes on the beach

      climb inside

           pull the lid shut tight

                turn the light off

Jo Surzyn lives in Norwich. Her work has appeared in *Lighthouse Literary Journal* and *The Bohemyth*. She was longlisted for the Café Writers Commission 2014, and since taking part in the Aldeburgh English Song Project she has started working on her first libretto.

KATIE SWINSON

Cathedrals

Hinge

Anxiety-Based Sex Education

The Block at Evening Time

Summer in Virginia

Cathedrals

He told me his mother took him
to visit cathedrals when he was small.
He talked about the mineral coldness of the marble
and his awe at the vaulted ceilings.
He said he wanted to learn Latin,
so he could read the inscriptions
carved into floor memorializing
the dead.

His cathedrals were succulent bait
and I was a naïve and hungry fish.
I salivated at the sound of his tender descriptions
while he pulled tighter at the hook,
that I was too busy being infatuated to feel.

When he finished reeling me in,
the hazy beauty of his cathedrals vanished.
He began to fiddle with the zipper
of my jeans and his mouth insisted
that I wanted to offer my body to him
as thanks for his poetic stories.

My mind snapped awake,
I was no longer a-dozing in the shallows.
I pulled away, no's rising up loudly from my mouth
while I moved further and further across the room.
But he had not gone to the trouble
of reeling me in just to let me go.

So he took my body,
and while I bled onto the sheets
he told me that this,
the violation and the pain,
was what I had wanted all along.
Waiting for his thrusts to cease,

I prayed to the God of his mother's cathedrals
for mercy.

Hinge

You are the aluminum wrapper
clinging to the piece of gum
I toss into my mouth. Your
shiny surface meets with
the filling in my back molar
shooting a sharp cringe through
my limbs. I shake my head
trying to escape the sensation.

You are the hinge of the door
where my forefinger is pinched
the pad swelling and rising into
a purple welt on my skin
where a perfect fingerprint
used to be.

You are the oddly pigmented mole
on my arm, growing rapidly.
I try and excise you, my melanoma,
but when I dig at your margins
you expand, rooting deeper
in my flesh.

You are the flashback
that startles me awake,
just as I was drifting off,
keeping me up until
I have prayed through
the Lord's Prayer
fifty times at least.

Anxiety-Based Sex Education

They took two sheets of construction paper
one blue, one pink
and cut them into hearts

    first comes love

they slathered Elmer's glue on each shape
and smacked them together,
leaving them to dry

    then comes marriage

this is sex (they said) and they pulled the hearts apart
leaving torn bits of color
dangling from each side

    then comes baby in the baby carriage

every person you have sex with
you are tearing off these scraps
and giving them away

    and then comes divorce

which means when you do meet
the right person, you can never
fulfill your part of the contract

    and then comes remarriage

    or a pilgrimage to an ashram

    disregard of everything holy

    a bad case of herpes

and sometimes even

a wish to put your heart back together

but you can't

so here – sign this pledge before the bell rings.

The Block at Evening Time

Two snakes mate in the backyard,
intertwined at the edge of the woodpile

while the peeping tom next door
counts the minutes until the lanes
between the houses go dark

and his favorite show begins.

Little girls, bare legged with bony knees,
charge up and down the concrete
squealing happily

and the widow's dog, who hates
children, yips and yaps like a smoke
alarm whose battery needs changing.

Thankfully, Donna, our neighborhood snitch,
isn't watching from her front window

to see my cat slip through her azaleas
and gleefully piss on her gray siding

but she'll know it was him anyway.

It's almost dark; the family with eight trashcans
filled with beer cans because they refuse
to recycle is finishing their game of horseshoes

which means it's time for my dad to leave for
the nightshift as the snakes untie their knot.

The deviant from next door emerges from his basement
and crosses the street to his favorite window where
he can watch the little girls get their baths

until Donna comes home and sees his shadow
in the moonlight and calls the cops on his sorry
ass once again.

Summer in Virginia

It's July and I can't sleep
because tomorrow
is the day you run back
to Chicago.

Our fingers are laced
and you're snoring like
an ogre king even
though you're only
twenty-two and skittish.

You're my hairy-backed
radiator, no need for quilts,
so warm I can smell your sweat
after you've just
had a shower.

Tomorrow we'll pack up
this damn twin bed
that knows our imprints
but wasn't meant for two.

I'll cry tomorrow,
so hard snot will run
from my nose and into
your mouth,

the mixture of salt and slime
will assure you that I'm already lonely,
but I've been craving this
exhale since April

ASSORTED POEMS

when you told me
giving someone else
a compliment takes
something away from you

and that your Ammy can
never know that you dated
a white girl because it could
literally kill her.

And that if I got pregnant
we'd have to get married
because your parents
couldn't live with anything less.

Which is why tomorrow
I'll sing all the way home,
ignoring my mascara streaks
and the crust on my upper lip.

Then I'll roll down the windows
letting in the heat to declare my
undying love for contraceptives

and call to future lovers
who might admit
they've held me
while we fell asleep.

Katie Swinson is from Charlottesville, Virginia and completed her undergraduate degree at James Madison University. She loves working with children, reading excessively and living near the Blue Ridge Mountains.

JAMES SYKES

The Beautiful Centre
No Connection
Frequent Visitor
Titles
Performance Piece
Android

ASSORTED POEMS

The Beautiful Centre

Close proximity triggered a kind of radiation sickness
but we continued to be drawn in by its soft glow,
a snaking parallel to the monochromatic.
Somehow it made things better, and perhaps
that was near enough. True understanding
would manifest as a kind of chalice: a buttery
sizzling juice within that would turn our teeth to ash.

No Connection

I will wear the robes: thicket-torn remnants
of my usual clothes. Enshroud me beneath
that sun-split canopy. I want to freeze
my fingers in a river and fill my head
with the names of species until I lose
the ability to touch-type. I want to hear
nothing but the mastered chirps and whispers
of the orchestra. Sneeze from the flowers.
Expose every allergy; unlearn them.
Return ozone-scented and muddy. Get dirty for it.

Frequent Visitor

It's not so much about moments succumbing
to the glacier-shift progress of positions
or kicking into 'life-changing' instantaneousness,
but rather how successfully you trump
the athleticism of the postmodern inner voice –
that intertwining headache
of competitor and commentator –
attention drawn to the structure of the marathon
rather than the abilities of the sportsmen.
And then as it looms hungry-wide –
the potential instant, the greatly-hyped event,
the action snaps to a stop: the shadow of something
boom mic-shaped, footsteps, and then, of course,
almost an echo – a familiar cough at the door.

Titles

At night he begins to tell you the names of stars.
You shush him but that's not quite enough
because the knowledge is still there; to you
his head is a beehive just out of earshot, secretly alive.

You like to splice the names of creatures
with moments of your life and give the stars
new titles: *the smoked-out kitchen iguana,*
the motorway-crash parakeet,
the kiss of the mayfly in the bus shelter.
That's silly, he says. I know, you reply,
thinking of him now under a different name.

In the morning: leftover pizza from the fridge –
the only reason you order takeaway
in the first place. If you could just deal
with the day's fanged associates while keeping
the newly-named stars in mind.
Pretend not to know how anything works.

JAMES SYKES

Performance Piece

Messaging you & walking through the party, smiling at people I haven't seen for a year / I'M SO ANXIOUS RIGHT NOW, I'M CHUGGING THIS DRINK, IT'S 'DARK FRUIT' OR SOMETHING, IT'S WEIRD, IT'S OKAY, I'M OKAY / someone asks what studying poetry is like / breathing exercises, death-thoughts, a little writing here & there, the memory-snort / 'good, yeah, difficult, a lot of poetry' / inexplicably become hyper-witty / feel like I'm stealing someone else's wi-fi / at the buffet table / feeling violent, feeling stupid, feeling ugly, feeling inappropriately erotic eating a falafel wrap / balancing the smile, levelling each eye's contact, swallowing the scream.

ASSORTED POEMS

Android

Dent my android head.
I need corrupting.

Vomit on my cataloguing system.
Clog it up with chunks.

I'm tacky and unconvincing,
rattling in a UFO from the 50s.

That's my clang of metal,
that's my ship's spooky hum.

That space is the distance
between me and an image of myself,

a photograph taken so long ago
it may as well be someone else.

James Sykes is currently a copywriter for a lawnmower company, which is pretty damn exciting, and has had poems published by *Black & Blue Writing* magazine and *Internet Poetry*. Important plans include: keeping up a cool blog, assisting in the destruction of the patriarchy, taking Manhattan and then Berlin, and of course, $$$$$$$$$.

REBECCA WHITE

30th July

November

The Garden

South West

This weekend

30th July

'We have eaten and loved and the sun is up,
we have only to sing before parting:
Goodbye, dear love.' *Basil Bunting*

We drank red wine
out of mugs
dressed in tree
finger cracks
smiled stained teeth
watched the candle
drenched in its own wet self
flicker
played Risk, Pontoon,
stripped, fucked, creaked
on the camp bed
and listened
to the roof
dressed in drumming
rain, hot we slept
woke each other up
and held on

waited for morning
us naked
and the birds dressed as birds.

November

It is a wet morning for a fire engine,
a wet one to be sat on the overpass
juggling for change,
or washing windows.

My love, I see you fifty years from now
holding yourself crooked on a cracked pavement,
one hand behind your back and the other
empty, by your side.

ASSORTED POEMS

The Garden

It is night time and I have gone to meet Grandma in the garden.
Your dyed auburn perm glistens and you wear lilac
and teach me a new word. The word tonight is
'inevitable'. This reminds my sleeping head
that the future that has not yet happened, that floats ahead of me until
morning wakes me and I am steeped in it, will occur.
Even as you talk the Superking in your hand is opening holes
in your heart, making tomorrow and all that comes after.
The thing, I realise, is that you know too, even now. Even now
when I am twelve and you are just retired and still painting your nails
to match the dresses that you sewed yourself. We are sat here now
and the lawn is perfectly mown but in the morning out of my window it
will be wild and peppered with dandelions
the flowers the golden craters of excitement I will feel behind my eyes
until I stop seeing versions of you in car parks, on buses.
For now, in the garden all your ghosts parade before us,
at Christmas singing, at Christmas coughing, at Easter hallucinating,
Christmas again crying, laughing I cannot tell and Easter again, dying.
When I wake the sun gasps and she is laughing her letters out of my drawer.

South West

I tried to stuff the landscape up my nose as I passed
hills that trapped the view and sheep
in fields of folded elbows and knees.

I wanted to be as close to this as to my memory
of the oysters that we bought and never ate
who lived in my fridge for two days before the bin.

I have shelled my hands, joints of balled flesh
in my fingers I am ready to tip my head back
and swallow the part of Wales that is already in my eye.

This weekend

I.

When I wake in the morning
the pieces that I remember best
are your face and your hands.

At night I can hear one
and feel the others on my back
but in the morning

you are herma. There are
no arms or legs and you roll
and roll cold stone.

II.

I get in sticky drunk
feet wet on bathroom tile
 eat half a tuna sandwich

and climb back into bed
after another evening
of missing you enough

to wonder if I could ease
back the scars knitting my wrists
and crawl inside to hide in my own arms.

III.

The next day I stare
with black eye
 eyes wet left.

REBECCA WHITE

Other faces
are pooling
and I hear them

discuss plans. I have
no plans
so I punch my head through glass.

The air on the other side
is blacker than my eyes
and it sticks to my skin.

I am drenching
and dripped
and swollen with the realisation that

I have found you at the back
not where I left you
closer than I thought.

Rebecca White has lived in Nottingham, Cardiff and Devon and will be adding her Creative Writing MA to a BA in English Literature and Archaeology. So is now qualified to write poems about museums, or excavate poems, or write poems about bones, in museums. realrvwhite.wordpress.com.